GOTHS

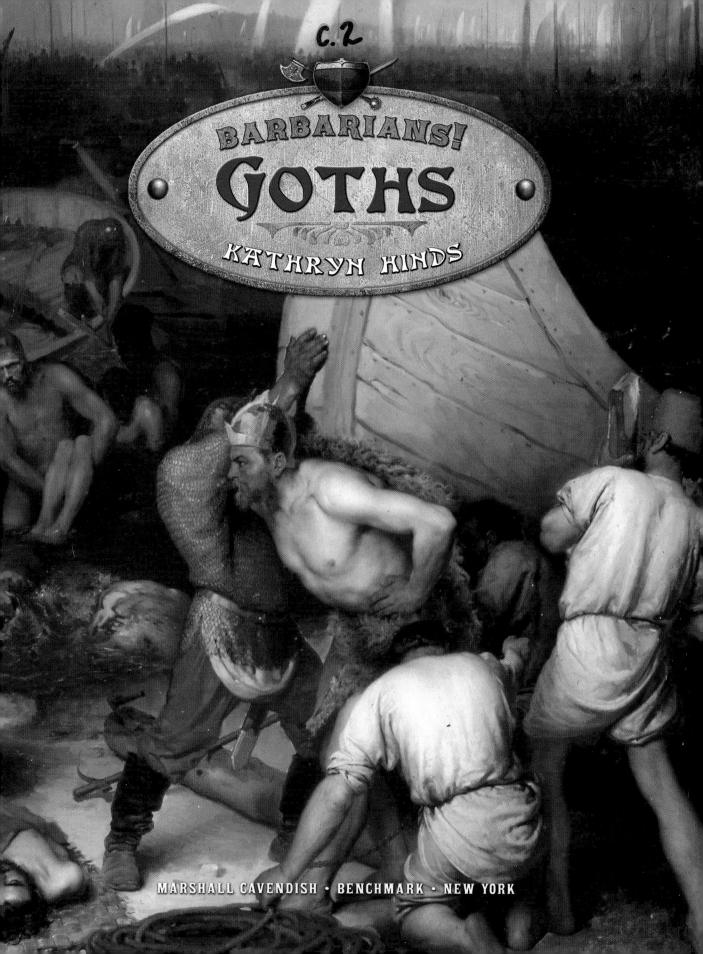

C.2

BARBARIANS!

GOTHS

KATHRYN HINDS

MARSHALL CAVENDISH · BENCHMARK · NEW YORK

To Donna and Larry

The author and publisher specially wish to thank Michael Kulikowski,
Professor of History at the University of Tennessee, Knoxville,
for his invaluable help in reviewing the manuscript of this book.

Marshall Cavendish Benchmark 99 White Plains Road Tarrytown, New York 10591
www.marshallcavendish.us
Text copyright © 2010 by Marshall Cavendish Corporation Map copyright © 2010 by Mike Reagan

Map by Mike Reagan

LIBRARY OF CONGRESS CATALOGING-IN-PUBLICATION DATA
Hinds, Kathryn, 1962-
Goths / by Kathryn Hinds.
p. cm. — (Barbarians!)
Includes bibliographical references and index.
Summary: "A history of the Goths, who rose as a power in the early third century and, under their famous
leader Alaric, succeeded in sacking Rome in 410."—Provided by publisher. ISBN 978-0-7614-4065-9
1. Goths—History—Juvenile literature. 2. Rome—History—Empire, 284-476—Juvenile literature. 3.
Migrations of nations—Juvenile literature. I. Title. D137.H56 2009 936'.00439—dc22 2009014114

EDITOR: Joyce Stanton PUBLISHER: Michelle Bisson ART DIRECTOR: Anahid Hamparian
SERIES DESIGNER: Michael Nelson

Images provided by Rose Corbett Gordon, Art Editor of Mystic CT, from the following sources: Cover: The
Granger Collection, NY Back cover: Werner Forman/Topham/The Image Works Page 1: AAAC/Topham/The
Image Works; pages 2-3, 61: Réunion des Musées Nationaux/Art Resource, NY; page 6: akg-images/British
Library; page 8: Vanni/Art Resource, NY; page 10: Scala/Art Resource, NY; page 12: The Art Archive/Museo
Nazionale Palazzo Altemps Rome/Gianni Dagli Orti; page 16: Hulton Archive/Getty Images; page 18: The Art
Archive/Archaeological Museum Istanbul/Gianni Dagli Orti; page 19: The Art Archive/National Museum
Bucharest/Alfredo Dagli Orti; pages 20, 24, 30, 40, 68: akg-images/The Image Works; page 23: National Geo-
graphic/Getty Images; page 25: The Art Archive/Tesoro del Duomo Monza/Gianni Dagli Orti; page 27: The Art
Archive/Abbey of Monteoliveto Maggiore Siena/Alfredo Dagli Orti; page 29: Universitetsbiblioteket, Uppsala,
Sweden; pages 33, 36: The Granger Collection, NY; page 41: Hermitage, St. Petersburg, Russia/Bridgeman Art
Library; page 42: The Art Archive/Museo Prenestino Palestrina/Alfredo Dagli Orti; page 45: Werner
Forman/TopFoto/The Image Works; page 47: Time & Life Pictures/Getty Images; page 49: Popperfoto/Getty
Images; page 51: Bridgeman Art Library/Getty Images; page 52: World History/Topham/The Image Works; page
54: Mary Evans Picture Library/The Image Works; page 56: Roger-Viollet/The Image Works; page 59: Bildarchiv
Preussischer Kulturbesitz/Art Resource, NY; page 60: Private Collection/Archives Charmet/Bridgeman Art
Library; page 63: Erich Lessing/Art Resource, NY; page 64: Lauros/Giraudon/Bridgeman Art Library; page 66:
The Art Archive/Museo della Civilta Romana Rome/Gianni Dagli Orti; page 69: AAAC/Topham/The Image Works.

Printed in Malaysia
135642

front cover: Alaric, one of the Goths' most famous leaders
half-title page: The tombstone of a member of the Gothic community in Spain, with the words *Recessit
in pace*—"Rest in peace"
title page: Returning from a raid, Goths carry their sick and wounded onto land, as imagined by a
nineteenth-century French artist.
back cover: Many Goths settled in Thrace, a region with a rich and ancient history of horsemanship
and metalworking.

CONTENTS

WHO WERE THE BARBARIANS?

THE HISTORY OF THE ANCIENT WORLD IS DOMINATED by the city-based societies of Greece, Rome, China, India, and others. Yet not far beyond the borders of these famed civilizations lived other peoples: the barbarians. They were first given this name by the ancient Greeks, imitating the sounds of languages that the Greeks found incomprehensible. Soon, though, barbarians came to be thought of not just as peoples unfamiliar with the languages and customs of Greece and Rome, but as wild, uncivilized, uncultured peoples. This stereotype has largely endured to the present day, and the barbarian label has been applied to a variety of peoples from many parts of Europe and Asia.

A Gothic soldier in Spain, armed with spear, sword, and shield

The barbarians, of course, did not think of themselves this way. They had rich cultures of their own, as even some ancient writers realized. The civilized peoples both feared the barbarians and were fascinated by them. Greek and Roman historians such as Herodotus and Tacitus investigated and described their customs, sometimes even holding up their simple values as a lesson for their own, more sophisticated societies. Moreover, the relationships between the barbarians and civilization were varied and complex. Barbarians are most famous for raiding and invading, and these were certainly among their activities. But often the barbarians were peaceable neighbors and close allies, trading with the great cities and even serving them as soldiers and contributing to their societies in other ways.

Our information about the barbarians comes from a variety of sources: archaeology, language studies, ancient and medieval historians, and later literature. Unfortunately, though, we have almost no records in the barbarians' own words, since many of these peoples did not leave much written material. Instead we frequently learn about them from the writings of civilizations who thought of them as strange and usually inferior, and often as enemies. But modern scholars, like detectives, have been sifting through the evidence to learn more and more about these peoples and the compelling roles they have played in the history of Europe, Asia, and even Africa. Now it's our turn to look beyond the borders of the familiar civilizations of the past and meet the barbarians.

INTRODUCING the GOTHS

T IS THE YEAR 410, AND THE GOTHS ARE SACKING ROME. Their leader, Alaric, has decreed that churches should be left alone and civilians should not be harmed. But the fact remains that the streets are full of barbarians, plundering the markets, the public buildings, and the homes of the rich—taking away everything of value that they can carry. No enemy army has set foot in the city of Rome in over eight hundred years. Yet here are the Goths, unstoppable. How have these barbarians become such a powerful force?

ORIGINS

Gothic power began to rise in the early third century. At that time the Goths lived in a region north and northwest of the Black Sea known to Greeks and Romans as Scythia. According to legend, however, the Goths had their beginnings far to the north. The sixth-century historian Jordanes, who was probably of Gothic descent, retold the old story:

Opposite page: In most conflicts between barbarians and the Roman Empire, the empire was the winner. This sculpture of a captured barbarian was part of a monument to Roman victory.

Now from this island of Scandza [Scandinavia], as from a hive of races or a womb of nations, the Goths are said to have come forth long ago under their king, Berig by name. As soon as they disembarked from their ships and set foot on the land, they straightway gave their name to the place. And even today it is said to be called Gothiscandza. Soon they moved from here to the abodes of the Ulmerugi, who then dwelt on the shores of the Ocean, where they pitched camp, joined battle with them and drove them from their homes. Then they subdued their neighbours, the Vandals, and thus added to their victories. But when the number of the people increased greatly and Filimer, son of Gadaric, reigned as king—about the fifth since Berig—he decided that the army of the Goths with their families should move from that region. In search of suitable homes and pleasant places they came to the land of Scythia. . . . Here they were delighted with the great richness of the country.

Jordanes concluded this episode, "so the story is generally told in their [the Goths'] early songs, almost as a history. Ablabius also, a famous chronicler of the Gothic race, confirms this in his most trustworthy account." Jordanes also said that he got much of his information from a history by Cassiodorus, a scholar who had worked for the Gothic king Theodoric, and from research of his own. Unfortunately, the works of Ablabius and Cassiodorus are now lost, so Jordanes's writings are as close as we can get to knowing how the Goths thought of their early history.

This depiction of the biblical prophet Ezra may actually be a portrait of Cassiodorus in his library—modern scholars have identified the books on the shelves in the background as texts that were known to belong to Cassiodorus.

The Goths' northern origins and travels south to the Black Sea may in fact be more legendary than historical. Modern archaeologists have not been able to prove any definite connection between the Goths and Scandinavia. There is evidence, however, that before the Goths occupied Scythia, people who shared a similar culture (shown in particular by certain types of burials) lived along the Vistula River, in what is now Poland. This was, in fact, right about where a Roman writer said a Germanic people called the Gutones lived during the first century. It is possible that these Gutones were ancestors of the Goths who settled north of the Black Sea.

In any case, it seems the Goths began to grow in power and importance during the second century. This was a time when the Roman Empire had pushed its borders to the edges of Germania and Scythia. These "barbarian" territories were occupied by many groups (often referred to as tribes) of Germanic-speaking peoples, as well as some groups of Iranian-speaking peoples known as Sarmatians.

The empire interacted with barbarian communities in a variety of ways. At centers along the frontier, or even deep inside barbarian territory, Roman merchants traded coins, wine, foodstuffs, and luxury goods for barbarian products such as furs and leather and amber, as well as for slaves. The imperial government supported friendly barbarian leaders near the frontier with money, gifts, and grain. The Roman military recruited young barbarian warriors to serve in the army.

Through such means, Roman coins, goods, and customs became known and desired far into barbarian lands. The empire, with all its riches and resources, was a constant source of envy and temptation. At the same time, it was a constant threat. Roman emperors held on to power mainly through control of the military. Therefore, to show their strength and keep up discipline in the army, they periodically sent expeditions across the frontier to "pacify" the barbarians. This way emperors could claim they were enforcing the borders and keeping the

A bearded Gothic warrior uses his shield to fend off Roman soldiers in a battle scene carved on a third-century marble tomb.

empire safe. Naturally these actions made the barbarians feel very unsafe. Moreover, Rome had a tradition of promoting conflict between different groups of barbarians, keeping them from threatening the imperial frontiers because they were too busy fighting each other.

The peoples of Germania and Scythia increasingly felt the need to band together in tribal confederations, groups that were large enough to give them security and strength to deal with the empire. The Goths can be seen as one such confederation, perhaps formed when the warrior leadership of several groups joined together for common defense. As this leadership achieved success, it attracted more followers, from a variety of tribal and ethnic backgrounds—all united by their shared need to stand up to Rome. The larger the confederation got, the more power and influence it had. And the longer it stayed together, the more it developed its own distinctive culture, which, like the confederation's main language, became known as Gothic.

EARLY ENCOUNTERS

The Gothic confederation may have been established in the area just north of the Black Sea by around 200. However, we don't get our first definite report of the Goths until 238. In that year, according to a Greek historian, a Gothic army raided the city of Histria on the northwestern coast of the Black Sea, near the mouth of the Danube River. The Roman border was vulnerable at this time because the empire was in the midst of ongoing civil wars, and many frontier troops had deserted their posts or been called away to fight elsewhere. The Goths (along with other barbarian confederations to the west) got very good at taking advantage of the empire's troubles. For many decades, nearly every time there was serious unrest in the empire, barbarians seized the opportunity to raid across its borders.

The next Gothic raid on record took place in 249. The 238 attack had happened close to the empire's northern border, the Danube. This

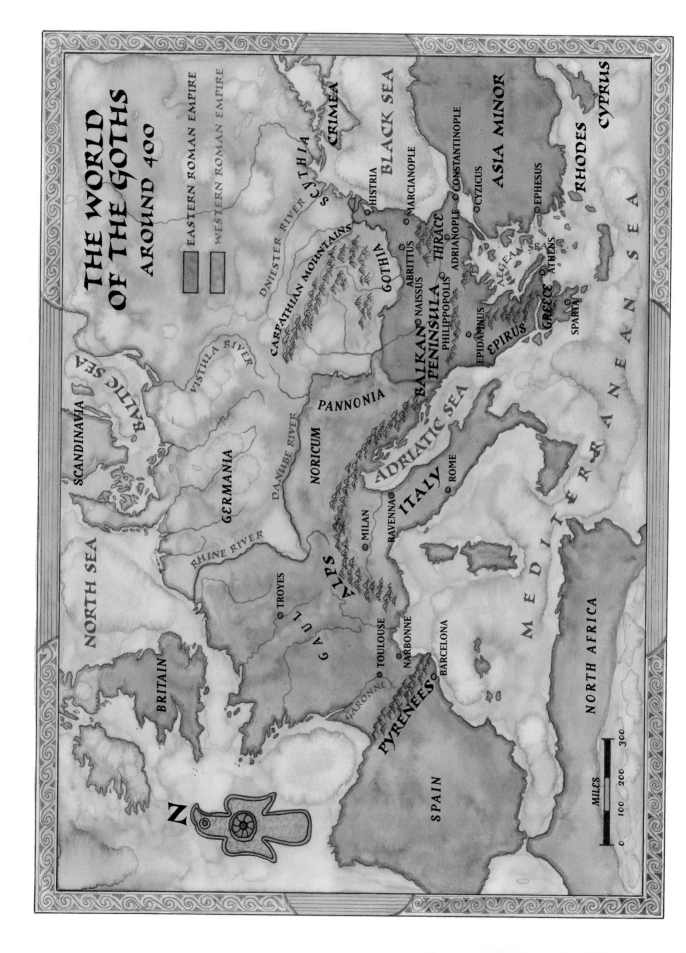

THE WORLD OF THE GOTHS
AROUND 400

EASTERN ROMAN EMPIRE

WESTERN ROMAN EMPIRE

N

NORTH SEA

BALTIC SEA

SCANDINAVIA

BRITAIN

GERMANIA

VISTULA RIVER

RHINE RIVER

DANUBE RIVER

GAUL

ALPS

TROYES

TOULOUSE

SARONNE

NARBONNE

PYRENEES

BARCELONA

SPAIN

NORTH AFRICA

NORICUM

PANNONIA

CARPATHIAN MOUNTAINS

DNIESTER RIVER

SCYTHIA

CRIMEA

BLACK SEA

GOTHIA

HISTRIA

MARCIANOPLE

ABRITTUS

NAISSUS

THRACE

ADRIANOPLE

CONSTANTINOPLE

CYZICUS

ASIA MINOR

EPHESUS

PHILIPPOPOLIS

BALKAN PENINSULA

EPIDAMNUS

EPIRUS

AEGEAN SEA

GREECE

ATHENS

SPARTA

RHODES

CYPRUS

MILAN

RAVENNA

ITALY

ROME

ADRIATIC SEA

MEDITERRANEAN SEA

MILES

0   100   200   300

time the Goths advanced a good deal farther. Under their leaders Guntheric and Argaith, they sacked Marcianople, a city that held a strategic position where two roads met a little way west of the Black Sea. The following year a Gothic force led by Cniva crossed the Danube much farther upstream and marched down into the Balkan Peninsula, plundering the countryside and towns along the way. Cniva's Goths captured a major city, Philippopolis, and spent the winter there. The emperor Decius led an army into the Balkans to try to drive out the Goths. But in 251 at Abrittus, a city west of Marcianople, Decius "was at once surrounded by barbarians and destroyed with a large part of his army," as an author of the early fourth century related.

We don't know what happened to Cniva after this, but we do know that over the next few years Goths continued to raid the eastern Balkan region known as Thrace. Then in the mid-250s, Gothic raiders took to the water, crossing the Black Sea in ships. In this way they attacked many cities on the northern and northwestern coast of Asia Minor. The Goths engaged in seaborne raids in the 260s and mid-270s as well.

Their greatest success as pirates came in 268–269. Joined by warriors from another barbarian group, the Heruli, they set sail with a huge fleet. After plundering the Black Sea coastline, they made their way through the strait that separated Asia Minor from Europe and crossed into the Aegean Sea. The force split into three parts. One, mostly Herulian, attacked the northern Balkans, but was soon defeated by the Roman army. Another group, primarily made up of followers of three Gothic chiefs, hit the islands of Cyprus and Rhodes, then turned to the western coast of Asia Minor, home to many rich cities. Before these Goths were forced back into the Black Sea by the Roman navy in 269, they even pillaged the temple of Diana* at Ephesus, one of the Seven Wonders of the World.

The third group, probably a mix of Goths and Heruli, ravaged Greece, striking such ancient and renowned cities as Athens and Sparta

*Goddess of women, the moon, and wild animals; known to the Greeks as Artemis

as well as plundering smaller towns and the countryside. These war-riors evidently left behind their ships and worked their way up the Balkan Peninsula mainly on foot. In 270 they reached the city of Naissus, where they were defeated by a Roman army led by the emperor Claudius II. Afterward known as Claudius Gothicus, he was the first emperor to take this title. His overwhelming victory resulted in the capture of so many prisoners of war that, according to a fourth-century biography, "the Roman provinces filled with barbarian slaves. . . . The Goth was made the tiller of the barbarian frontier, nor was there a single district which did not have Gothic slaves in triumphant servitude."

A slave gathers harvested grain into an oxcart on a Roman farm.

Claudius's successor, Aurelian, also earned the title Gothicus. He crossed the Danube to defeat a large Gothic force led by a king named Cannobaudes, whom he captured. It was said that five thousand Goths died in battle, although this number is probably exaggerated. It must have been an impressive victory all the same, for roughly a hundred years later the historian Ammianus Marcellinus wrote,

"Defeated by Aurelian—that brave man, the avenger of their mis-deeds—they [the Goths] kept peace for many centuries." This was an overstatement, but the Danube frontier did remain mostly safe from the Goths for several decades.

Not all Goths known to the Romans were slaves or enemies. Gothic units had been serving in the Roman army for some time. After the raid on Histria in 238, the empire made a peace treaty with the Goths, prom-ising them annual payments so long as they withdrew from Roman ter-ritory and returned Roman prisoners of war. The treaty may also have required the Goths to supply the empire with troops. In any case, Gothic warriors were part of a Roman army that went to war (and suffered defeat) in Persia in 242.

From this point on, many Goths would fight for Rome. The warriors could gain wealth and prestige, while the empire gained skilled fight-ers at a time when it was getting harder and harder to recruit Roman citizens into the army. From the Roman point of view, using Gothic mercenaries paid off in another way. It removed many of the most war-like men from the frontier, so they would be less likely to cause trou-ble for Rome—especially if they ended up getting killed in battle.

THE RISE OF THE TERVINGI

The Gothic confederation appears to have been a fairly loose-knit asso-ciation. Different groups of Goths had their own chiefs or kings, who often operated independently of one another. The Greeks and Romans knew the names of some of these leaders, such as Cniva and Can-nobaudes. But as far as we can tell, they were unaware of specific groups or subgroups of Goths till almost the end of the third century.

In 291 a Roman speech made the first mention of the Tervingi, described as *pars Gothorum*—"a section of the Goths." The Tervingi had been fighting alongside a people called the Taifali against other Ger-manic groups, the Gepids and a division of the Vandals. This conflict apparently took place somewhere around the Carpathian Mountains, not too far north of the Danube. The fighting in the region evidently made Rome nervous, or perhaps even spilled across the border, because the emperor Diocletian led a campaign against the Tervingi and Taifali, whom he defeated. (They had already overcome the Gepid-Vandal coalition, thanks to their "better cause and greater cleverness," in the words of Jordanes.)

Despite this setback, the Tervingi became more and more powerful. Although they were not mentioned again for some years by Roman writers, we know that other peoples in the region were in upheaval, pushing against the Danube frontier. The most logical explanation is that the Tervingi were expanding their domain.

The emperor Diocletian strengthened Rome's frontier defenses, which included building new forts and enlarging old ones along the Danube.

Rome did not try to interfere with this process. Perhaps as a result of a treaty made after Diocletian's victory, the Tervingi seem to have become valued allies. They apparently supplied troops for the empire's continued warfare in Persia, while also providing security against other barbarian groups that might threaten Rome's borders. In any case, by the 320s the Tervingi dominated much of the lower Danube. Roman writers soon began to refer to the north bank of the river as *ripa Gothica*, "the Gothic bank." A Greek writer was the first to call the region Gothia, a name that caught on with the Romans and with the Goths themselves.

In 328 the emperor Constantine ordered the building of a bridge across the Danube and the construction of new forts along the river. This show of strength may have been due to the fact that during a civil war earlier in the decade, Gothic troops had fought on the side of Constantine's enemy. Moreover, the Tervingi were continuing to increase their power, pushing west toward the great bend in the Danube River

Roman soldiers were also engineers and construction workers when necessary. This is part of a detailed sculpture that shows the Roman army building bridges and fortifications.

(in modern-day Hungary). In about 330, Sarmatians living near the Danube bend asked for Rome's help to stop the Tervingi expansion. Constantine launched a war against the Tervingi, whose leader was named Ariaric.

Constantine's oldest son led the Roman army across the Danube and, according to Jordanes, drove thousands of Tervingi from their settlements to starve and freeze to death. In 332 Constantine made a treaty with the Tervingi, who had to send hostages—including Ariaric's son—to Rome to guarantee peace. Probably the Tervingi also agreed to supply recruits for the Roman army and to pay tribute to the Roman emperor.

The bishop who wrote Constantine's biography in 337 stated, "The Goths finally learned to serve the Romans." But the treaty must have had benefits for the Tervingi, too, because they kept the peace for thirty years. They also continued to feel a sense of personal loyalty to Constantine and his family. According to one Roman writer, describing the situation under Constantine's successor, the Tervingi "treated our emperor as if he were theirs."

LIFE in GOTHIA

THE REGION THAT BECAME KNOWN AS GOTHIA HAD AT ONE time been the Roman province of Dacia. Even though the empire gave up trying to control this territory in the third century, many people still lived there who had embraced the Roman language (Latin) and way of life. The Goths who moved in brought with them their own language and customs, but they seem to have made little or no effort to interfere with their romanized neighbors' lifestyles. Even though the Tervingi came to dominate these former Roman subjects, they must have had many peaceful interactions with them. In fact, there was much about Roman culture that the Goths admired, and the longer they were in contact with it, the more aspects of it they imitated or adapted.

VILLAGES, CRAFTS, AND TRADE

Gothia was a region with numerous rivers, large and small, that watered rich countryside, perfect for growing grain and other food crops. There were also nearby grasslands, the western edge of the great band of

Opposite page: A nineteenth-century painting of a swamp near the Danube illustrates the abundant wildlife found in the fertile lands occupied by the Goths.

21

steppe that stretched across Asia and into central Europe. These plains were home to nomads who herded cattle, sheep, and horses. Nomad camps could be found in Gothia, and there was frequent interaction between nomads and farmers.

Farm families made up the majority of the population. They lived in villages near the rivers, with only a couple miles separating one settlement from another. An average village was home to around a dozen households, who raised not only crops but livestock. Cattle were the most important animals, followed by sheep or goats. Few if any villagers had horses, though, which were generally limited to especially wealthy and powerful people.

Village houses were typically arranged in rows. They were built of wood or wattle-and-daub and partially—sometimes almost completely—dug into the ground. With the surrounding earth as insulation, these houses kept cooler in summer and warmer in winter than would have been possible otherwise. Nevertheless, houses built entirely aboveground could also be found in Gothia. Such homes combined living space for both people and animals all under one roof. This way the animals were protected from harsh weather, and their body heat helped warm the house.

Most cooking was probably done over a central hearth in clay pots. The staple foods were wheat, barley, and millet. They could be boiled into porridge or ground into flour to make bread. Each household probably ground its own grain in a hand mill—a labor-intensive process that was usually part of women's work. Besides food preparation, women also would have been responsible for making nearly all their family's clothes, which were generally woven from wool.

Gothic villages seem to have been largely self-sufficient, producing most of the everyday items people needed. Tools of wood and iron were generally locally made, as were clay pots. The best-quality pots were thrown on a potter's wheel. Additional things made in Gothia included jewelry, particularly bronze or silver brooches and buckles, and combs and other objects crafted from antler or bone.

Sometimes such items were produced in centralized locations—for example, archaeologists have excavated a village with nearly twenty buildings in which combs, assembled from several pieces of antler, were in the process of production. At another settlement, archaeologists found a fourth-century glass factory. There must have been a high demand for its products, for they have been found at sites from Norway to Ukraine.

The fact that there was a percentage of the population who did not need to support themselves by farming but could specialize in skilled crafts shows that Gothia was fairly prosperous during this time. An important element of Gothic prosperity was trade with the Roman Empire. Rome seems to have valued this trade, too, since the entire lower Danube frontier was opened to it—a great contrast to the past, when the empire had allowed only a few, carefully controlled, frontier crossings for merchants.

Archaeologists have discovered large numbers of Roman bronze coins in Gothia, especially in settlements within twenty or so miles of the Danube. The residents of this border zone, at least, appear to have enthusiastically adopted the use of money (although they may also have continued the more traditional practice of bartering for goods). The local people even produced their own bronze coinage, imitating Roman models. Among the Roman imports purchased in Gothia were wine and perhaps olive oil, as shown by finds of large clay jars called amphorae, which were used to transport these liquids.

Amphorae like this one were used by both Greeks and Romans to transport and store wine, olive oil, and fish sauce. The clay jars varied in size: most were about a foot and a half tall while some stood as high as five feet.

ELITE GOTHS

Roman imports were part of the lifestyle of the Gothic elite. Along with wine, the homes of high-ranking Goths were graced by elegant Roman pottery and glassware. Large gold Roman coins became medallions to adorn many of Gothia's aristocrats.

Gothic craftspeople, too, produced luxury items for the elite, such as gold brooches, sometimes inlaid with thin slices of garnet in intricate designs. Leatherworkers and metalworkers made bridles and other gear for the horses ridden by high-ranking Goths. Smiths forged helmets and swords for the leading warriors. (The average Goth went into battle with just a spear and a wooden shield.)

Archaeologists have found only a few sites that may have been the headquarters of Gothic leaders. Among these are the remains of three fortified settlements situated along important trade routes northwest of the Black Sea. All of them were much larger than the average Gothic village and had stone walls or foundations. One showed clear signs that it had been surrounded by a ditch and a rampart of earth, and apparently it had also been guarded by three towers.

At another site, along the Dniester River, archaeologists have found a walled village with eight houses, a pottery workshop, and an unusual central building. This large structure—whose purpose is unknown—featured a row of Roman-style columns and was also roofed like a Roman building, with clay tiles. Moreover, it had glass windows. Scholars can only conclude that it was built by some wealthy and powerful Goth who had spent time in the Roman Empire and brought back an admiration for its architecture.

An eagle-shaped brooch once worn by a high-ranking Goth. Eagles were popular Gothic emblems; the Goths adapted the design from the eagles used as symbols of the Roman Empire.

Historical records do not give us enough information to know how much of an aristocracy or noble class existed in Gothia, nor can we know how formal or rigid any Gothic class system was. We are not even entirely sure how the Goths were governed. Greek and Roman writers referred to several Gothic leaders as kings. The Latin word *rex* is related to the Gothic term *reiks*, and both have been translated as "king." But while for the Romans a *rex* was an absolute monarch, the Goths of this time seem to have used *reiks* to mean a distinguished man or, in general, a leader—but not someone with sole governing power in all circumstances.

It may be that a *reiks* had command over a certain number of men who were bound to him by family relationships and personal ties of loyalty. He may have had real authority only during wartime, while in everyday life he had to rely more on the power of persuasion to get his followers to do as he wished. Whether or not a *reiks* inherited his position or was chosen by some kind of assembly of warriors is an issue that scholars have not settled. Perhaps in some Gothic groups at some times leaders were elected, while in other times and places inheritance was the normal practice. Or perhaps *reiks* was not even a formal rank among many of the Goths, but simply a title used to honor prominent and influential men.

In addition to kings, the Tervingi had a leader whom the Romans called a judge (*iudex* in Latin). The Gothic title for this person was *thiudans*—the word one later Gothic writer chose when he translated Greek *basileus*, meaning "emperor." This use of the term shows that

This silver sculpture of a hen and chicks was a gift to an Italian church by a sixth-century Gothic queen named Theodolinda.

the Tervingi's judges ranked higher than their kings. We also know the Tervingi could have a number of kings at the same time, but apparently only one judge. Although Greeks and Romans regarded the judge as the leader of the entire Tervingi, we don't actually know just how much authority he had. We also can't be sure how he was chosen, although the position may have been passed down from father to son.

THE COMING OF CHRISTIANITY

Ancient authors wrote very little about Gothic religion. From what they did record, we gather that wooden images sometimes represented the deities, who included a god of war. As in most ancient cultures, worship might involve sacrificing animals, who provided the meat eaten at religious feasts. Some of these feasts evidently celebrated seasonal holidays.

The Goths encountered Christianity through their contact with the Romans. The new religion had spread throughout the empire during the first and second centuries. By the time of the Gothic raids on Asia Minor in the mid-200s, Christianity was well established in many communities there. Not surprisingly, then, Christians were among the people taken captive during the raids. These Christians continued to practice their religion among the Goths, and they also passed it on to their descendants, who may well have intermarried with the Goths in some cases. Moreover, the Christians taught their beliefs to the Goths they lived with. Philostorgius, a fifth-century church historian, tells us, "They converted many of the barbarians to the way of piety and persuaded them to adopt the Christian faith."

In 313 the emperor Constantine gave Christianity legal recognition. It was still a minority religion in the Roman Empire, but by the 320s he was favoring it over other faiths. A Christian himself, he may have influenced some of the Tervingi to adopt Christianity when they made peace with him in 332. In any case, a leader of Gothia's Chris-

tian community soon rose to prominence. His name was Ulfila, Gothic for "little wolf."

We do not know how Ulfila got his education, but he knew Gothic, Latin, and Greek, and was said to have written religious works in all three languages. Sometime between the late 330s and 341 he was chosen by the Tervingi judge to go on a diplomatic mission to the emperor Constantius II (Constantine's son) in Constantinople. While there, he was made "bishop of the Christians in the Gothic land"—that is, he was put in charge of all the priests and churches of Gothia.

Ulfila fulfilled this responsibility for seven or eight years, but then, according to Philostorgius, the Tervingi judge conducted "a tyrannical and fearsome persecution" against the Christians. The reasons for this may have been more political than religious, since Christianity was

Gothic Christians meeting with a group of monks, as imagined by a sixteenth-century Italian artist

always closely associated with Roman power—the leaders of the Tervingi may have suspected that Gothic Christians were more loyal to Rome than to their own people. In any case, Ulfila and much of the Gothic Christian community left Gothia and were granted land inside the empire by Constantius himself. There they were known for generations afterward as the *Gothi minores*, or "little Goths."

Once settled in his new home, Ulfila began the work that made him most famous: the translation of the Bible into Gothic. This was a huge endeavor, for the Bible had been translated into only a couple of languages at this point, both of which had long been in literary use. But Gothic had never really been written down before. Philostorgius described Ulfila's achievement: "He was the inventor for them [the Goths] of their own letters," which he had to create first before he could even begin to write his translation. Ulfila did, however, leave out the Old Testament books of Kings. Philostorgius explained why: "These books contain the history of wars, while the Gothic people, being lovers of war, were in need of something to restrain their passion for fighting rather than to incite them to it." Indeed, the little Goths became known as "peace-loving and unwarlike" shepherds. But as we shall see, other groups of Goths were far from giving up warfare.

A GOTHIC PRAYER

THE LORD'S PRAYER, WHICH JESUS TAUGHT TO HIS DISCIPLES IN THE GOSPEL ACCORDING TO Saint Matthew, became one of Christianity's most important prayers. Here is the Gothic version from Ulfila's Bible. (The English translation accompanies each line so that you can compare the two languages.)

Atta unsar thu in himinam (Our Father who art in heaven)

weihnai namo thein (hallowed be thy name)

qimai thiudinassus theins (thy kingdom come)

wairthai wilja theins (thy will be done)

swe in himina jah ana airthai (on earth as it is in heaven).

Hlaif unsarana thana sinteinan gif uns himma daga (Give us this day our daily bread)

jah aflet uns thatei skulans sijaima (and forgive us our trespasses)

swaswe jah weis afletam thaim skulam unsaraim (as we forgive those who trespass against us)

jah ni briggais uns in fraistubnjai (and lead us not into temptation)

ak lausei uns af thamma ubilin (but deliver us from evil)

unte theina ist thiudangardi jah mahts jah wulthus in aiwins (for thine is the kingdom and the power and the glory forever).

Above: *The silver cover, made in the 1660s, of the only surviving copy of Ulfila's Gothic Bible. The book itself was copied out in Ravenna in 520, with silver and gold letters written on purple parchment.*

UPHEAVAL

I N THE 360S, DECADES OF PEACE BETWEEN ROME AND GOTHIA came to an end, in large part because of troubles within the empire. In 364 the army chose as emperor one of its generals, Valentinian, who made his brother Valens co-emperor. The next year the imperial brothers decided to split their domain into halves (an arrangement that would become permanent over the course of the following decades). Valentinian took control of the Western Empire, which he would rule not from Rome but from Milan, in northern Italy. Valens ruled the Eastern Empire, with its capital at Constantinople (modern Istanbul, Turkey). Since the dividing line between the two realms was in the west of the Balkan Peninsula, it was Valens who now had to deal with Gothia.

VALENS AND ATHANARIC

Valens was still getting settled on his throne when a man named Procopius tried to take it from him. Although not directly descended from Constantine, Procopius belonged to the same family and claimed the

Opposite page: A fourth-century gold medallion portraying the brothers Valentinian and Valens, joint rulers of the Roman Empire

31

right to rule on that basis. According to ancient historians, the Tervingi agreed with him (or at least said they did) and sent three thousand of their warriors to fight on his side (for which they received ample payment).

The judge of the Tervingi at this time was Athanaric, "the most powerful man of the tribe" according to Ammianus. Many scholars think his father was Ariaric's son, the one who had gone to Rome as a hostage as part of the 332 treaty with Constantine. Whether or not this was true, it seems Athanaric had been wanting to renegotiate the treaty, and that may have been one of the real reasons behind the Gothic support of Procopius.

After Procopius was captured and killed in 366, Valens had Procopius's Gothic troops rounded up and held prisoner in Thrace. The Greek historian Eunapius recorded that Athanaric "demanded back these noble warriors. The case was embarrassing and difficult to settle justly." We don't know for sure what ever became of the warriors, but we do know what Valens did next: he declared war on the Tervingi.

In 367 Valens led his army across the Danube. There were no real battles, though, because Athanaric had his people make a strategic withdrawal into the mountains. The next year the emperor intended to try again, but heavy rains and severe flooding made any serious military action impossible. Instead Valens set his soldiers to building and restoring fortresses along the river. The following year Valens and his army once again invaded Gothia, and this time Athanaric met them in battle.

The Goths were defeated, but Athanaric was neither captured nor killed, and apparently considered fighting on. However, all trade with Rome had been cut off since the war's beginning, and the bad weather in 368 had destroyed the Goths' crops. The people were running low on food and other necessities. After some thought, Athanaric asked for a peace settlement, and Valens agreed to meet with him.

Athanaric, however, refused to cross the Danube—he was, Ammianus tells us, "bound by a most dreadful oath, and also forbidden by the strict commands of his father ever to set foot on the Roman territory." At the same time, the Romans felt "it would be unbecoming and degrading for the emperor to cross over" to Athanaric. So a compromise was agreed on, and Valens and Athanaric each got into a boat with a few followers and were rowed into the middle of the river. A senator named Themistius was present and reported,

Valens was so much cleverer than the man who spoke for the barbarians that he undermined their confidence in him. . . . All the same, having thrown his opponent he then set him on his feet once more, stretched out his hand to him . . . and made him a friend before witnesses. . . . And so [Athanaric] went away highly contented, in the grip of contrary emotions: at once confident and fearful, . . . cast down in spirit by those aspects of the treaty in which he had lost his case but exulting in those in which success had fallen to him.

Athanaric and Valens meet in the middle of the Danube.

The Romans left Gothia, taking Tervingi hostages with them, and allowed trade to resume in a couple of locations. But the war and the compromises afterward had hurt Athanaric's reputation among many of his people. Although the Tervingi now had peace with Rome, they did not have peace among themselves. For one thing, the fifth-century historian Socrates tells us, Valens began to send Christian missionaries into Gothia. Athanaric seems to have looked on these men as Roman spies; at the very least, they were spreading Roman influence. Along with many other Tervingi lords, Athanaric regarded Gothic Christians as a threat and started persecuting them.

Yet other elite Tervingi embraced Christianity, creating discord at all levels of society. One of the highest-ranking converts was a king named Fritigern, who opposed Athanaric so strongly that the two were soon at war, according to Socrates. The fact that Roman soldiers were sent to help Fritigern must have made Athanaric even more hostile to Romans and Christians alike. But a still greater threat was now looming.

REFUGEES

The Tervingi were not the only large group of Goths at this time. To the east, north of the Black Sea, were the Greuthungi. Their ruler was Ermanaric, "a most warlike king and, on account of his many and various deeds, feared by the neighbouring peoples." A new people, however, had come to the neighborhood, and they didn't fear Ermanaric in the least. They were the Huns, who "made a sudden incursion into the extensive and fertile districts" of the Greuthungi. Ammianus, writing about twenty years later, recorded that Ermanaric "was astonished at the violence of this sudden tempest, and although . . . he long attempted to hold his ground, he was at last overpowered by a dread of the evils impending over his country" and "gave himself up to a voluntary death."

Ermanaric's successor, Vidimir, was killed in combat after a number of battles. Vidimer's son Videric was the next king, but he was only a young child. Two prominent warriors, Alatheus and Saphrax, acted as his regents. Deciding they could no longer resist the Huns' advance, they led their followers in retreat to the Dniester River. This apparently brought them to the edge of Tervingi territory. Ammianus continues the story:

> When Athanaric . . . had become informed of these unexpected occurrences, he prepared to maintain his ground, with a resolution to rise up in strength. . . . At last he pitched his camp at a distance in a very favourable spot near the banks of the Dniester . . . and sent [scouts] to reconnoitre the approach of the enemy; while in the mean time he himself, without delay, marshalled his troops in line of battle. However, things turned out in a manner very contrary to his expectations.

The Huns had also sent out scouts, so they knew all about the Gothic forces. During the night they crossed the river farther north, then turned south to sweep down on the Tervingi. Taken by surprise, Athanaric lost many of his men in the battle, and he and the survivors only saved themselves by retreating into the nearby mountains. Athanaric then withdrew deeper into his territory and began to erect fortifications. But he had already lost too much authority. In Ammianus's words, "The greater part of the population which, because of their want of necessaries, had deserted Athanaric, resolved to flee and seek a home remote from all knowledge of the barbarians [the Huns]; and after long deliberation . . . they resolved that a retreat into Thrace was the most suitable."

The events narrated by Ammianus probably occurred over the course of several years, but there are no definite dates till 376. This was when a large number of Tervingi—tens of thousands, probably—gathered by the Danube under the leadership of Fritigern and another king, Alavivus. They sent a message to Valens, asking permission to settle in Thrace, "promising to live quietly, and to furnish a body of auxiliary troops if any necessity for such a force should arise." At the time Valens, along with most of his army, was in Syria, his base for a war against Persia. It took several months for negotiations and for messengers to go back and forth between Syria and the Danube, but the Tervingi refugees got their wish.

The Romans' plan was to ferry teenage boys over first so that they could serve as hostages to guarantee the good behavior of their people. Next the adult men were supposed to come across, leaving behind their wives and young children. Many of the men, however, paid bribes to Roman officials so that their families could cross with them. The Goths had good reason to fear leaving them behind: numerous unprotected women and children were illegally transported across the Danube—kidnapped, in fact—by Roman soldiers and officials. According to Eunapius, these Romans "simply put, . . . had all decided to fill their houses with domestics and their land with shepherds and to exploit the situation in order to satisfy their every desire."

Even without such abuses, the situation was extremely difficult and dangerous. The Danube was a mile or more wide, and its waters were swollen from heavy rains. Many of the ferries were makeshift rafts and

A Gothic family defies Roman rules to cross the Danube together.

boats that fell apart or overturned in the river. Some people were too panicked to wait for their turn to be taken across and tried to swim. Between the unsturdy vessels and the swimmers fighting the strong river currents, there must have been a large number of drownings. Meanwhile, those still waiting to cross coped with fear, crowding, and unsanitary conditions.

It took days for all the refugees to finally get to the Roman side of the Danube. Once there, things didn't improve. The Roman officials in charge of resettling the Tervingi held back food and other supplies, instead selling them for high prices for their own profit. Then, says Ammianus, "those detested generals conceived the idea of a most disgraceful traffic." They rounded up dogs and sold them to the Goths to eat. The price? One dog in exchange for one child, who would become a slave. The refugees were growing desperate, and it must have seemed to many parents that even a life of slavery would be better for their children than starvation.

As the year 377 dawned, the Tervingi were no closer to settling on the new lands promised them by the emperor. With food still scarce and little shelter against freezing temperatures, unrest in the refugee camps grew. Not only that, but the Greuthungi led by Alatheus and Saphrax had given up on holding their position at the Dniester and now swarmed the north bank of the Danube. They, too, wanted admittance to the empire. Their request was denied, but they did not go away. Finally, in early spring, the Roman commander Lupicinus decided it would be best to move the Tervingi to the area around his headquarters in Marcianople.

In the hubbub of getting the relocation under way, Roman officials left the Danube bank unguarded. Alatheus and Saphrax seized the opportunity to lead their people across on rafts. When Fritigern learned of this, he slowed the Tervingi's march to Marcianople as much as possible, "to allow time for other powerful kings to join him." It would be good to have an alliance with the Greuthungi leaders in case the situation with Lupicinus went from bad to worse. Fritigern was right to be worried.

THE GOTHIC REVOLT

When the Tervingi neared Marcianople, Lupicinus invited Fritigern and Alavivus to a dinner party. Most of their people remained camped outside the city, which they were not allowed to enter, not even to purchase food and supplies. Before long rioting and fighting broke out, and the Tervingi killed and robbed many of the soldiers guarding the city walls. Ammianus tells us,

> When Lupicinus learned by a secret message that this had happened . . . he put to death all the attendants of the two leaders. . . . When the [Goths] who were besieging the walls heard this news, . . . they gradually increased their number to avenge their kings, who, as they thought, had been detained by force. . . . And since Fritigern was quickwitted and feared that he might be held with the rest as a hostage, he cried out that they [the Romans] would have to fight with heavy loss of life, unless he himself were allowed to go out with his companions to quiet the people.

Fritigern was permitted to go, leaving Alavivus behind, either dead or held hostage (ancient authors never mention him again). The next day Tervingi warriors began to raid the countryside around Marcianople. Lupicinus hastily gathered his troops and marched out to put down the uprising. Nine miles from the city, Fritigern's forces surprised the Romans, defeating them in a furious and bloody battle.

The Tervingi's victory inspired others to join them—not only the Greuthungi but also discontented Roman subjects, such as impoverished peasants, overtaxed miners, and escaped slaves. (It was a source of particular joy that among the runaways were many of the Tervingi enslaved the previous year.) Soon Gothic units serving in the Roman army deserted and came over to Fritigern's side, too. From this point on in Ammianus's history, he stops calling Fritigern's followers the Tervingi: they were now "the Goths." And they "spread over every quarter of Thrace, while their prisoners or those who surrendered to them pointed out the rich villages, especially those in which it was said that abundant supplies of food were to be found."

Despite several confrontations with Roman forces, the Goths continued to pillage Thrace. Valens decided he would have to end the Gothic rebellion himself. Having wound up affairs in Syria, he returned to Constantinople on May 30, 378. He spent a couple months preparing his army, and finally led it out against the Goths at the beginning of August.

The emperor's scouts soon reported on the location of the enemy, who were sheltering inside a huge circle made up of the wagons in which their families and possessions traveled. The scouts estimated that Fritigern had ten thousand warriors. Valens had at least twice that many soldiers, so he confidently set up camp outside the city of Adrianople. On August 8 a Christian priest sent by Fritigern arrived with an offer to negotiate peace, but Valens refused. The next morning he went out to meet the enemy.

It was a hot day, and the Romans had to march eight miles from their camp to the Goths'. Now they discovered that the scouts had been wrong, and Fritigern had at least as large an army as Valens did. Nevertheless the Roman units took their positions facing the Goths, who ranged themselves in front of their wagon circle. Then Fritigern again offered to negotiate.

Valens was seriously considering Fritigern's proposals when two of the Roman units surged forward and came to blows with the Goths. Disorder followed, increased by the arrival of Gothic cavalry who had been away foraging for provisions.* The horsemen, "descending from the mountains like a thunderbolt, spread confusion and slaughter among all whom in their rapid charge they came across." The battle had begun.

*This cavalry included a group of Alans (an Iranian people) and Huns who had allied with Fritigern the previous year.

A family loads their oxcart in preparation for moving out to seek new lands. The father, armed and mounted on his horse, exchanges farewells with a couple of neighbors. Other villagers carry on with their daily tasks: on the left a man draws water from a well, while on the right a young woman grinds grain in a hand mill.

The fighting raged all afternoon. At last, Ammianus wrote, the Romans "were entirely beaten back by the overpowering weight of the barbarians, and so they took to disorderly flight, . . . each man trying to save himself as well as he could." The Goths pursued them till darkness fell, so that by day's end two-thirds of the Roman army had been killed. Among the dead was Valens himself.

For the next few years bands of Goths roved through the Balkans, plundering the countryside. The new East Roman emperor, Theodosius I, succeeded for a time in driving them out of Thrace, but they simply raided other areas instead, including Pannonia (part of modern Hungary) and northern Greece. At last, in October 382, Theodosius made peace with the Goths. Historians are not sure what all the terms of the treaty were, but the Goths did finally receive some of the lands they had wanted ever since they decided to cross the Danube.

Themistius explained the peace settlement to his colleagues in the Senate this way: "Philanthropy has prevailed over destruction. Would it perhaps have been better to fill Thrace with corpses instead of farmers? The barbarians are already transforming their weapons into hoes and sickles and cultivating the fields." Although Themistius exaggerated, it did seem to him and many others that the Goths were no longer a threat. But then there were the words of Bishop Ambrose of Milan, who had warned shortly after the Battle of Adrianople, "This is not yet the end."

MEANWHILE, NORTH OF THE DANUBE

Part of the Crimean coastline, in what is now southern Ukraine. The Crimea became home to some eastern Goths during the Huns' expansion.

ALTHOUGH NUMEROUS TERVINGI and Greuthungi fled into the Roman Empire after the coming of the Huns, many other Gothic groups stayed behind. Athanaric and the Tervingi loyal to him settled in the Carpathians. Even after Athanaric left them, most of this group remained in this mountainous region.

Another group of Goths north of the Danube seems to have been ruled by a queen for a time, probably after her husband died. Her name was Gaatha, and in the mid-380s she transferred power to her son, Arimir. She and her daughter, Dulcilla, then left Gothia and journeyed to Cyzicus, on the northwestern coast of Asia Minor. They took with them the remains of twenty-six Gothic Christians who had been burned to death during the persecutions around 370. Once Gaatha saw the remains given respectful burial, she returned to Gothia, while Dulcilla remained in Cyzicus. The twenty-six martyrs became saints honored by all Gothic Christians.

During the first two decades of the 400s, large numbers of Huns seem to have settled down in Gothia. By this time most Goths remaining north of the Danube and the Black Sea had either joined the Huns as willing allies or had been conquered by them. As subjects, the Goths were expected to provide their rulers with both farm products and fighting men. Many Goths broke away the moment the Hun empire began to collapse in 453, but other groups of Goths continued to fight under the command of Hun leaders until around 470.

Some eastern Goths may have escaped Hun rule completely. To do so, however, they apparently had to move into what is now southernmost Ukraine. Archaeological finds in the Crimea, the peninsula that juts down into the Black Sea, show that Goths began living in this area in the fourth century. In the sixth century, the historian Procopius wrote about the Crimean Goths as an independent community. Although their independence didn't last, their language did—a form of Gothic was still spoken in the Crimea well into the sixteenth century.

INSIDE the EMPIRE

THE EMPIRE HAD ALLOWED MANY IMMIGRANT GROUPS TO settle in its territory, but usually only after they had made a complete surrender. Normal Roman practice then was to break up the immigrant community, sending many of the people to work as slave laborers or tenant farmers on various estates, drafting large numbers of men into the military, and expecting the rest to pay their taxes and adopt Roman ways as quickly as possible. But nothing like this happened to the Goths covered by the treaty of 382.

The Goths remained free, and the lands they farmed were theirs, not some Roman landlord's. Although they were naturally not allowed to set up a Gothic kingdom within the empire's borders, they had their own communities, their own leaders, and seem to have enjoyed some degree of independence from the Roman government. They may even have been exempt from paying taxes. In any case, they kept many of their traditional customs and a sense of their identity as Goths.

In return, the empire got a steady supply of soldiers. A great many

Opposite page: A second-century mosaic portrays a gathering of Roman soldiers. Over the next two centuries, more and more of the Roman army would be recruited from among barbarian peoples, including the Goths.

43

Gothic men—more than ever before—joined the Roman military. Some enlisted in permanent auxiliary units. Others were mercenaries hired as needed, in which case imperial officials usually negotiated with a Gothic commander to lead his personal followers on the empire's behalf. And, for the first time, a significant number of high-ranking Goths began to serve as officers in the Roman army. Unlike the commoners who were usually recruited, these men, according to Eunapius, "were paramount in reputation and nobility."

GOTHIC GENERALS

The Gothic leaders Fritigern, Alatheus, and Saphrax had apparently died sometime between 380 and 382. In 381 Athanaric, the Tervingi judge who had remained north of the Danube, broke his old oath, made his peace with the empire, and crossed into Roman territory. Theodosius himself welcomed Athanaric to Constantinople, where he died just two weeks later. The old generation of leaders was gone, but new men of "reputation and nobility" were rising to prominence.

For example, two Gothic generals named Fravitta and Eriulf were of such high rank that they were the emperor's dinner guests on at least one occasion. During this banquet, however, they had a violent quarrel. They fought, and Fravitta killed Eriulf. Knowing that Eriulf's family would demand vengeance and a feud would start, Fravitta left the Gothic community for good. Theodosius gave him a command in the regular East Roman army, in which Fravitta went on to a successful career. He even married a Roman wife, and was still remembered a hundred years later as "a barbarian by birth, but for all the rest a Greek,* not only in his habits, but also in his character and his religion."

The end of this statement tells us that Fravitta had embraced the worship of the ancient Greek gods and goddesses. Theodosius, however, was a Christian. He followed the version of Christianity that would

*The writer uses *a Greek* to mean "one of us," indicating that Fravitta became fluent in Greek, the main language of the Eastern Empire.

come to be called Catholicism, and which he had made the empire's official religion. But since he greatly valued Fravitta's skill as a general, he did not force the Gothic warrior to change his faith.

Some Christian emperors before Theodosius had promoted another form of Christianity, often known as Arianism. The main difference had to do with the relationship between Jesus and God. In Catholicism, Jesus was God the Son and was, in a mystical sense, exactly the same as God the Father—both were equally divine (as was God the Holy Spirit). In Arianism, Jesus was still God's son and still divine, but was created by God the Father and therefore inferior to him. The issue was a huge controversy during the fourth century; there were even riots and persecutions because of it.

This silver portrait of Theodosius was made in honor of his tenth year as emperor.

Most Gothic Christians were Arians and refused to be swayed to Catholicism. This was one of the factors that made many people in the Eastern Empire uncomfortable with the presence of such a large number of Goths among them. Moreover, Gothic warriors had a reputation for fearsome violence. Synesius, a North African landowner who visited Constantinople during Theodosius's reign, remarked, "Only a madman wouldn't be afraid of seeing all these young men, who have grown up in foreign lands and still live according to their customs, charged with carrying out military activity in our country."

Then there were the Gothic commanders, some of whom rose to positions of great influence. Synesius complained about incidents

> when one dressed in animal skins gives commands to others wearing the chlamys [a short Greek cloak], and when a man takes off the fur coat that covered him, dons the toga, and joins the Roman magistrates to discuss the items on the agenda. . . . And then, as soon as such a man as this leaves the Senate chambers, he immediately puts on his furry clothes again, and when he meets his fellows, they all laugh about the toga. If you've got one of those things on, they say, you can't draw your sword.

Synesius was emphasizing a stereotype, but he was not exaggerating the resentment he (and others like him) felt about the Goths.

All the same, the empire was depending more and more on barbarian soldiers to defend it. After a Roman general named Magnus Maximus mutinied and took over much of the Western Empire, a large part of the army Theodosius led against him was made up of Goths and other barbarians. The churchman (and future saint) Jerome was dismayed by this trend: "Just as in the past, there was indeed nothing stronger and solider than the Roman empire, so now . . . there is nothing weaker, for whether we fight civil wars or foreign wars, we need the help of various barbarian peoples."

Even more Goths apparently served in Theodosius's next war, against another usurper in the West. The conflict reached its climax in September 394 in a two-day battle in the borderlands between Italy and the Balkans. Theodosius placed a huge Gothic force in the front ranks, where they endured the fiercest fighting. According to the historian Orosius, half the Goths—ten thousand men—were killed that day. On the second day Theodosius and his remaining army won the battle. Orosius said that Theodosius had achieved a double victory, since he had both defeated the usurper and gotten rid of so many Goths.

We will probably never know if Theodosius purposefully put the Goths in the vanguard in the hope they would take major casualties. But it seems likely that many Goths suspected this was the case. They knew that the more military manpower they lost, the harder it would be to keep the privileges they had enjoyed since the 382 treaty. In any case, discontent was growing, and one Gothic leader was about to do something about it.

REBELLIONS

In January 395 Theodosius died unexpectedly in Italy, leaving his sons as emperors of the East and West. Neither was ready to rule, however, so each had a regent in charge of the government and army. The Western Empire's regent was the powerful general Stilicho. One of his first acts was to order the surviving Gothic units to go back to the East.

The commander of one of those units was a young man named Alaric. He was, we can guess, angry about the way the Goths had been treated during and after the recent battle. Since they had fought so hard and sacrificed so much to win Theodosius's war, he felt they should have been better rewarded. In particular, he believed he should have been given a promotion: a high rank in the Roman army, not just command over his own Gothic followers. Alaric, who had been a child when his people crossed the Danube in 376, wanted not just to live in the empire but to be part of its power structure.

Back in the Balkans, Alaric led his men in a revolt. He was soon joined by many more followers—not only Goths but also escaped slaves and

An early-nineteenth-century artist imagined Alaric looking much like a German military officer of the time.

other disaffected Roman subjects. They raided the suburbs of Constantinople and then invaded Greece. A hundred years later the historian Zosimus described this foray: "They immediately began to pillage the country and to sack all the towns, killing all the men, both young and old, and carrying off the women and children, together with the money. . . . [W]hatever countries of Greece the Barbarians passed through . . . were so ravaged, that the traces are visible to the present day."

In 397 Stilicho, who claimed Theodosius had made him regent of the East as well as the West, led an army into Greece to put down the rebellion. This move into the Eastern Empire threatened to undermine the regent in Constantinople, and he had Stilicho declared a public enemy. Moreover, he opened talks with Alaric, whom he saw as the lesser of two evils. As a result, he awarded Alaric an official Roman military command in Greece. For the time being, this was enough to satisfy Alaric and his followers.

Other discontented Gothic leaders may have been inspired by Alaric's success. The next one to make a move was Tribigild, who commanded warriors from a Gothic community in Asia Minor. These Goths were possibly the survivors of a group of Greuthungi who had entered the empire in 386. The immigrants who were not killed in fighting after they crossed the Danube were taken captive, resettled as farm laborers, and made to live under Roman law; many of their young men were drafted into the military.

In 399 Tribigild and his followers defeated the first Roman army sent against them. The second army to confront Tribigild was commanded by another Goth, Gainas. He decided to use the conflict to gain power for himself. As the price for dealing with Tribigild, he demanded the Eastern regent be replaced. He got his way, but then marched to Constantinople to demand more, including a military office like Alaric's. Even that was not enough, and Gainas started working to make himself the power behind the Eastern throne. But one of his rivals struck back, forcing Gainas to flee Constantinople in July 400. The next day a mob killed thousands of the city's Gothic residents—mostly women and children.

A Roman army commanded by Fravitta pursued and defeated Gainas. He escaped and fled across the Danube with his remaining followers. The Goths' old territory, however, was now home to a growing population of Huns. Before long, Gainas was killed by the Hun leader Uldin, who sent his head to Constantinople and as a result became (for a time) a Roman ally. By now Tribigild had died in battle in Thrace, so this round of Gothic uprisings was over.

THE LURE OF ITALY

After the events of 399–400, the new East Roman regent apparently decided to back out of the 397 agreement with Alaric. In any case, the Eastern Empire no longer seemed very hospitable to Alaric's Goths, and he decided they should go west to find a new home. In November 401 they reached the Italian border, and Alaric issued a set of demands to Stilicho. Not getting what he wanted, he invaded Italy the following spring.

After several inconclusive battles, Alaric and his followers retreated into the northwestern Balkans. Stilicho turned his attention to other problems. Unrest was growing in Britain and along the empire's Rhine River frontier. Stilicho knew he was eventually going to need major military assistance. In early 405 he offered Alaric an official Roman command. Having accepted, Alaric moved his Goths into

An illustration from 1753 shows Stilicho meeting with Gothic ambassadors, one of them fancifully depicted wearing a winged helmet.

Epirus (present-day Albania), ready to be called into action when Stilicho summoned him.

Then a new crisis arose. Late in 405, a previously unknown Gothic king named Radagaisus emerged from central Europe and crossed the Alps into Italy. It took until August 406 for Stilicho, aided by Hun auxiliaries, to defeat and kill him. The Romans and Huns enslaved thousands of Radagaisus's followers.

Another crisis struck the Western Empire at the end of that year, when a large number of Vandals, Alans, and Suevi* crossed the frozen Rhine and invaded Gaul. Stilicho was occupied with this and other problems well into 407. By then Alaric was tired of waiting for action. His men were restless—they had not received the pay promised by Stilicho, and they had already pillaged the surrounding region too much to get any more supplies from it. So Alaric led them into Noricum (modern Austria) and sent a message to Stilicho. He demanded four thousand pounds of gold, or he would invade Italy.

Stilicho decided to make the payment, but he was fast losing power. In May 408 the Western emperor Honorius had him arrested and executed. Stilicho's supporters in Rome and other Italian cities were also killed, including the families of all the barbarian auxiliaries serving in Stilicho's army. One result of this tragedy was that these barbarian soldiers—thousands of them—fled to join Alaric in Noricum.

Alaric and his newly enlarged army marched down into Italy and besieged Rome. His following continued to grow, as thousands of escaped barbarian slaves—in particular, the survivors of Radagaisus's invasion force—flocked to him. Alaric now commanded as many as 40,000 men. Daunted by the huge army outside their walls, and fearful of starvation, the people of Rome asked for a truce. Alaric granted it, especially since the Senate paid him 30,000 pounds of silver, 5,000 pounds of gold, 3,000 pounds of pepper, 4,000 silk garments, and 3,000

*Like the Vandals, the Suevi were a Germanic group.

scarlet sheepskins—plenty of loot for him to share out to his army.

Then Alaric entered into negotiations with the emperor, who was staying in Ravenna in northeastern Italy. Alaric offered Honorius an alliance in exchange for a fixed annual payment of gold and grain, together with a permanent grant of lands where he and his followers could control access to Ravenna and the eastern mountain passes into Italy. Alaric also wanted to be made supreme commander of the West Roman military, as Stilicho had been. Honorius agreed to the gold and grain, but not the rest.

Ships enter Ravenna's harbor in a scene from one of the splendid mosaics that adorn the city's churches.

Alaric came back with a counteroffer, as described by the historian Zosimus:

> Alaric did not now want office or honour, nor did he now wish to settle in the provinces previously specified, but only the two Noricums, which are on the far reaches of the Danube. . . . Moreover he would be satisfied with as much corn [grain] each year as the emperor thought sufficient, and forget the gold. . . . When Alaric made these fair and prudent proposals, everyone marvelled at the man's moderation.

It seems that what Alaric most wanted was a lasting peace between his people and the empire. But Honorius turned down his compromise.

In this second-century sculpture, Roman cavalrymen slaughter Germanic barbarians in battle. By Alaric's time, however, the empire could no longer count on its ability to defeat barbarian armies.

In 409 Alaric besieged Rome again. Then he set up a puppet emperor, a senator named Priscus Attalus. But although Attalus gave Alaric supreme military command, he slighted the Goths in other ways and was generally ineffective. Alaric deposed him in July 410, and once more prepared to negotiate with Honorius.

Events took a new turn, however, while Alaric awaited the emperor at the meeting site several miles from Ravenna. Sarus, a Gothic general in Roman service, led a small force in a direct attack on Alaric. Outraged, Alaric turned his back on the negotiations and marched on Rome. On August 25 he and his followers entered the city and spent three days sacking it.

The Goths went away with dozens of wagonloads of loot. But Alaric still had not achieved either the official recognition and position he desired for himself or the secure homeland he wanted for his people. He had thought his threats to Rome would persuade the emperor to give in to his demands. He had no way of knowing that Honorius simply didn't care that much about the ancient city, which was no longer the real power center of the empire. It remained, however, a potent symbol. To many people, Alaric's sack of Rome seemed like the end of civilization. As Saint Jerome lamented, "The whole world perished in one city."

THE CHURCHMAN PELAGIUS, IN ROME WHEN THE GOTHS SACKED IT, LATER RECALLED
the feelings of the panic-stricken citizens: "Rome, the mistress of the world, shivered,
crushed with fear, at the sound of the blaring trumpets and the howling of the Goths.
. . . Every household had its grief and an all-pervading terror gripped us." Writing in
the sixth century, the historian Procopius summed up the sack this way: "They set
fire to the houses which were next to the gate [through which they had entered] . . .
and after plundering the whole city and destroying the most of the Romans, they
moved on."

Other authors, however, tell a different story. Very few buildings were burned or
damaged in any way. Alaric did not want to destroy the city. But since he had not gotten what he wanted from the emperor, he needed loot to reward his followers' loyalty.

*Above: For centuries, Alaric's sack of Rome has been seen as an episode
of uncontrolled violence and destruction.*

He designated two large churches as refuges, where Rome's citizens could wait in safety while the Goths ransacked their houses. There were even instances of Goths escorting wealthy women, unharmed, to these havens.

Alaric was a Christian, and he ordered his men (many of them also Christians) to be especially careful not to hurt priests or nuns, and not to take any precious objects that were used in church services. In one case reported by Orosius, an old woman handed over gold and silver vessels belonging to one of the churches, telling a Gothic soldier, "Now you must look after them since I can't." Alaric found out about this and

HOW BAD WAS THE SACK OF ROME?

organized a procession to return the vessels, which were solemnly carried between a double line of guards with their swords drawn, while "Romans and barbarians in concert raised a hymn to God in public."

In spite of all this, there was no doubt violence and suffering, though far less than would normally happen during the sacking of a city. At the same time, Rome had ruled much of the known world for centuries, so the sack made a huge psychological impact on people. And it shook their faith. Worship of the ancient Roman gods had been outlawed in 391, but there were still numerous pagans, believers in the old religion. To many of them, Rome had brought the sack on itself by abandoning its traditional ways in favor of Christianity. Christians struggled to understand how God could have allowed the Goths to invade their city, and wondered what terrible sins they were being punished for.

The sack of Rome inspired the North African bishop (and later saint) Augustine to begin his monumental work *The City of God*, in which he explained that Christians really did not belong to any earthly city—not even Rome—but to the eternal Heavenly City. Another Christian author, though, writing in 417, took the Western Empire's barbarian troubles as a call to action: "If any mental energy remains, let us shake off the servile yoke of sin. . . . Let us not fear, because we have collapsed in flight in a first contest, to take a stand and embark on a second battle." Similar feelings were expressed in the very same year by the pagan poet Rutilius Claudius Namatianus, who had been an official in Rome and witnessed its recovery after the sack:

Let thy [Rome's] dire woe be blotted and forgot;
Let thy contempt for suffering heal thy wounds . . .
Things that refuse to sink, still stronger rise,
And higher from the lowest depths rebound.

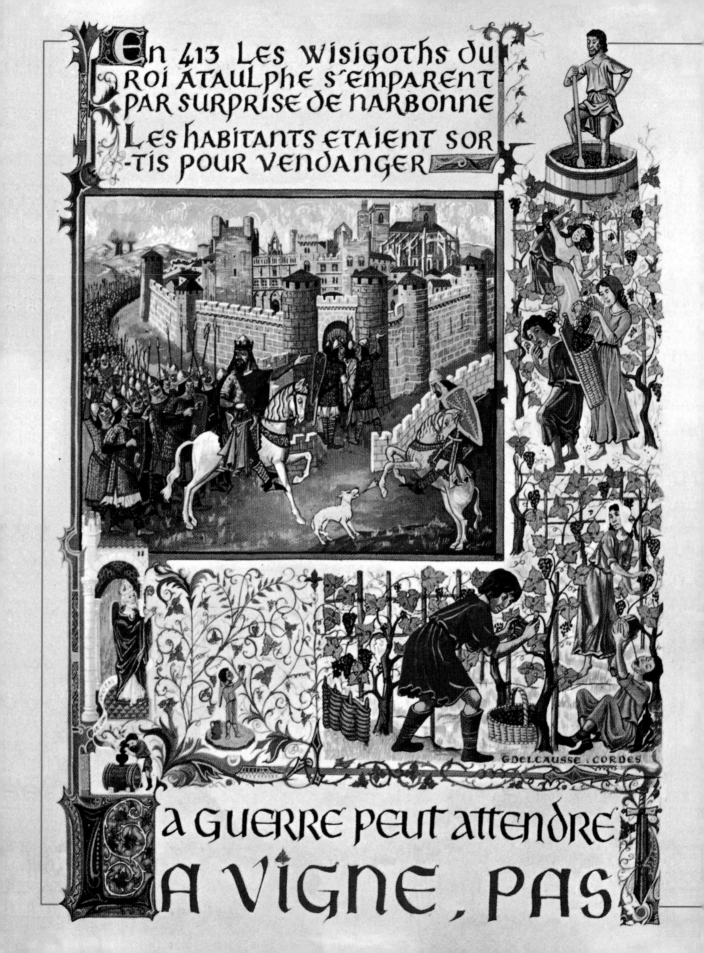

En 413 Les Wisigoths du Roi Ataulphe s'emparent par surprise de Narbonne Les habitants étaient sor -tis pour vendanger

La guerre peut attendre La vigne, pas

BARBARIAN KINGDOMS

ALARIC DIED JUST A COUPLE MONTHS AFTER THE SACK OF ROME. Leadership of his Goths passed to his brother-in-law, Athaulf, who decided Italy could no longer support them. In 411 he led the Goths into Gaul. There he became involved in Roman power struggles, backing a Gallic nobleman who had proclaimed himself emperor of the West. When Athaulf dropped his support in 413, the usurper had to surrender to the imperial authorities—only the might of the Gothic army had ever given him a chance of success. The Goths now settled down around the city of Narbonne, where Athaulf hoped they would be a force to be reckoned with.

GOTHIC GAUL

Athaulf supposedly explained his ambitions to one of Narbonne's leading citizens, who reported:

> It seems that at first he [Athaulf] ardently desired to blot out the Roman name and make all the Roman territory a Gothic empire.

The Goths under Athaulf take the city of Narbonne while its people are out in the countryside harvesting grapes from the vineyards.

. . . Having discovered from long experience that the Goths, because of their unbridled barbarism, were utterly incapable of obeying laws, and yet believing that the state ought not to be deprived of laws . . . he chose to seek for himself at least the glory of restoring and increasing the renown of the Romans by the power of the Goths, wishing to be looked upon by posterity as the restorer of the Roman Empire.

This may be why Athaulf decided to marry the emperor Honorius's sister Galla Placidia, who had been taken hostage during the sack of Rome. (Zosimus reports that the Goths treated her "with all the honour . . . due to a princess.") The wedding took place in 414; the historian Olympiodorus described the festivities:

Placidia, dressed in royal raiment, sat in a hall decorated in the Roman manner, and by her side sat Athaulf, wearing a Roman general's cloak and other Roman clothing. . . . Along with other wedding gifts, Athaulf gave Placidia fifty handsome young men dressed in silk clothes, each bearing aloft two very large dishes, one full of gold, the other full of precious . . . stones, which had been carried off by the Goths at the sack of Rome.

Later that year the couple had a son, whom they named Theodosius after Placidia's father. Since Honorius had no children, Athaulf and Placidia's child could be regarded as the rightful heir to the West Roman throne.

This dream was never realized. Young Theodosius died in early 415. He was buried in Barcelona, Spain, because the Roman general Flavius Constantius had cut off the Goths' access to supplies and forced them out of Gaul. Some of the Goths began to lose confidence in Athaulf, and that summer he was assassinated.

After a brief power struggle, a man named Wallia (or Vallia), emerged as the Goths' leader. He made peace with Constantius, who gave the Goths enough grain to feed 15,000 warriors and their families. In return the Goths handed over hostages from among their nobles and sent Placidia back to her brother—who soon married her off to Constantius. (A troop of Goths went with Placidia when she married Constantius, and they loyally guarded and supported her for the rest of her life.)

In 416 the Goths went to war "on behalf of the Romans." Their task was to drive out the Vandals and Alans who had taken over much of the Iberian Peninsula. The campaign lasted two years, at the end of which few if any Vandals or Alans remained in southern Spain. Constantius called an end to the fighting and rewarded the Goths' success with a grant of "land for farming" along the Garonne River in southwestern Gaul. Wallia, however, died before his people could settle in their new home.

Theoderic I now became the Goths' king, making his headquarters the city of Toulouse. As his people established themselves in their new territory, they came to be known by a new name: the Visigoths. *Visi* meant "good," "wise," and/or "noble." It was a proud name for a people who were achieving both security and power. Under Theoderic's leadership, the Visigothic domain came to be an almost completely independent kingdom within the Western Empire.

In return for their land grant, the Visigoths were expected to defend the empire from its enemies. For several years they found themselves fighting large gangs of bandits as well as the Vandals and Alans who remained in northern Spain. By the 430s, however, the Visigoths felt

A fifth-century ivory plaque portrays Galla Placidia and her son by her second marriage. He became emperor of the West at the age of six, with Placidia ruling as his regent for the next eight years.

strong enough to challenge the empire for control over more of southern Gaul. In 436 they launched a rebellion, during which they besieged Narbonne. The Romans were able to break the siege only with the help of a large Hun cavalry force. But in 439, outside Toulouse, the Visigoths captured the Roman commander and killed all the Huns under his command. A peace settlement was reached after this, and the Visigoths barely appear in history again till 451.

In that year, under the leadership of Attila, the Huns invaded Gaul. The Roman army needed all the help it could get and called on the Visigoths to fulfill their defense agreement. Theoderic led his warriors north and met Attila's forces on a plain near the city of Troyes in a combat known as the Battle of the Catalaunian Plains. The Gothic historian Jordanes described the fighting in heroic terms: "Hand to hand they clashed in battle, and the fight grew fierce, confused, monstrous, unrelenting—a fight whose like no ancient time has ever recorded. There such deeds were done that a brave man who missed this marvelous spectacle could not hope to see anything so wonderful all his life long."

The Visigoths won the day, but Theoderic died in the battle. He was succeeded by his son Thorismund, who ruled for two years before he was killed by his younger brother Theoderic II. His reign lasted until 466, when he was murdered by the remaining brother, Euric. By this time the Franks, another Germanic people, were making serious inroads into northern Gaul, taking advantage of instability at the West Roman court. Not to be outdone, Euric, Jordanes tells us, "becoming aware of the frequent changes of [Western] Roman Emperor, . . . pressed forward to seize Gaul on his own authority."

By 476 Euric had control of most of southern Gaul. Within another decade he had extended his rule over northeastern Spain. But soon after Euric's son Alaric II came to power in 484, the Franks began to push into southwestern Gaul. In 507 Alaric was killed in battle against the forces of the Frankish king Clovis, and the Visigoths lost nearly all their Gallic territory. The Visigothic realm in Spain, however, grew into a flourishing kingdom. It survived until 711, when it was overcome by invading Arabs from North Africa.

A nineteenth-century French artist painted this scene of the Frankish king Clovis triumphantly entering the city of Tours after defeating the Visigoths.

THE EASTERN GOTHS

As we saw on p. 41, many Gothic groups did not migrate into the Roman Empire in the fourth century but remained north of the Danube. During the fifth century several of these groups came under the rule of the Huns. In 453 Attila died, and the empire he had built collapsed. The Huns' subjects began to break free, but it was a complicated process that took roughly a decade. During this period Attila's sons waged two wars against a group of Goths based in Pannonia, whom they regarded as deserters. Both times the Huns were soundly defeated.

These were not the only battles the Pannonian Goths had to fight. There were power struggles, often violent, for leadership of the group. The winner was a member of the Amal family named Valamer, who founded a dynasty of rulers. Valamer did not last long, however, thanks to warfare with other ex-subjects of the Huns. He was killed in combat by the Sciri, a Germanic people. This led to a great battle between the Goths and the Sciri and their allies; Jordanes describes the outcome:

> The party of the Goths was found to be so much the stronger that the plain was drenched in the blood of their fallen foes and looked like a crimson sea. Weapons and corpses, piled up like hills, covered the plain for more than ten miles. When the Goths saw this, they rejoiced with joy unspeakable, because by this great slaughter of their foes they had avenged the blood of Valamer their king.

In 473 Valamer's brother led the Pannonian Goths into the western Balkans. He died the next year, and was succeeded by his son, Theodoric. In the following years a rivalry developed between Theodoric's Goths and the Goths living in Thrace, whose leader was another Theodoric, nicknamed Strabo ("the Squinter"). Much of the conflict was promoted by the Eastern emperor, Zeno. As a Greek historian imagined Strabo saying, "While remaining at peace, [the Romans] wish the Goths to wear each other down. Whichever of us falls, they will be the winners with none of the effort, and whichever of us destroys the other side will . . . be left with diminished numbers to face Roman treachery." Realizing this, the two Gothic groups reached a temporary agreement not to fight each other.

Theodoric next attacked the outskirts of Constantinople, then went raiding through the Balkans. In 479 he captured Epidamnus, a city on the coast of the Adriatic Sea. Three years earlier the last emperor of the West had been deposed and sent into exile by a Germanic king named Odovacar. Now Theodoric offered Zeno six thousand troops to help the East Roman army take back Italy—or to overthrow Strabo's Goths. Zeno did not take him up on either offer, so Theodoric stayed where he was and bided his time.

Theodoric, in a mosaic from Ravenna. The barbarian king was a great patron of the arts, learning, and religion.

Strabo died in an accident in 481. During the upheaval that followed, Zeno seems to have taken the opportunity to move against the Thracian Goths, and Theodoric left Epidamnus to pillage the southwest Balkans. Apparently he did so much damage that Zeno was persuaded not only to make peace with him in 483 but to give him high appointments in the army and government. The following year the Thracian Goths joined forces with Theodoric's Goths. This united people would become known as the Ostrogoths (*ostro* meant "eastern").

Zeno soon began to doubt Theodoric's loyalty and took back his military command. Theodoric rebelled, and in 487 he marched on Constantinople and cut off part of the city's water supply. The two leaders had reached a stalemate. The best way to break it, they decided, was for Theodoric to go to Italy.

The Ostrogoths reached Italy in August 489. They spent the next three years alternately battling Odovacar and besieging his capital, Ravenna. In early 493 both sides were worn down and ready to negotiate. Ten days after they agreed to share power, Theodoric killed Odovacar during a banquet. With a stroke of his sword, the king of the Ostrogoths became the king of Italy.

Theodoric was not just a bloodthirsty warrior, however. At the age of eight he had gone to Constantinople as a royal hostage and lived at the imperial court until he turned eighteen. He had been educated in Greek and Roman culture, which he deeply respected. As he said in a letter to the emperor in 508, he had "by Divine help learned in Your Republic the art of governing Romans with equity. . . . Our royalty is an imitation of yours, modelled on your good purpose, a copy of the only Empire."

This mosaic in a Ravenna church patronized by Theodoric shows part of his splendid palace.

Theodoric had come to Italy not to destroy it, but to restore its glory. During his thirty-three-year reign, he repaired defenses and public buildings in many cities. He built a new palace and churches in Ravenna. He studied philosophy and asked Cassiodorus, a very cultured Roman and high-ranking official, to give him a list of books that would help him become an ideal philosopher-king.

Moreover, he instilled these same values in his daughter Amalsuntha, who was said to be wise, fair-minded, strong-willed, and fluent in Greek and Latin as well as Gothic.

After Theodoric died in 526, Amalsuntha ruled the Ostrogoths as regent for her young son. The boy lived for just eight more years, however, and Amalsuntha could only hold her throne by asking a male cousin to reign at her side. Less than a year later he had her killed, even though she was under the protection of the Eastern Roman emperor Justinian.

The murder gave Justinian a reason to declare war against the Ostrogothic kingdom. It was a long, arduous, bloody process, but in 561 he completed the reconquest of Italy. Only seven years later, though, the Lombards (another Germanic group) swept into Italy and destroyed Justinian's hopes for a reunited empire. Yet seeds had already been sown and were starting to grow, destined to flower into a variety of cultures that were blends of Roman and barbarian. The Western Empire was dead—but modern Europe was being born.

LETTER FROM A GOTHIC QUEEN

AFTER HER SON'S DEATH, AMALSUNTHA KNEW THE GOTHIC WARRIOR ELITE would not tolerate being ruled by a woman for long. She decided to make her cousin Theodahad her co-ruler, a decision she explained in a letter to the Roman Senate. Events would prove that Theodahad did not deserve the praise she gave him, but the letter remains an excellent example of Amalsuntha's values, eloquence, and determination.

> After mourning for the death of our son, of blessed memory, our concern for the people's common good had conquered a dutiful mother's heart, so that it dwells not upon the cause of her own grief but upon your prosperity. We have searched into the kind of help we might obtain to strengthen the kingdom's administration. . . .
>
> We have chosen by God's grace the blessed Theodahad as the consort of our reign, so that we, who have until now borne in solitary deliberation the burden of the commonwealth may now carry out the achievement of all things by united counsels.

Above: A sculpture of a young woman living in Italy during the time of Amalsuntha gives an impression of how the Gothic queen herself may have appeared, since the hairstyle was in fashion during her reign.

We shall be seen to be two persons in mutually working out the administration of the State, but one person in purpose. . . .

Rejoice, Fathers of the Senate, and commend to the heavenly powers what we have accomplished. We have desired to do nothing blameworthy, we who have . . . commanded all things to be put in order. We of course preserve with liberality the kingdom's tradition, since one who is demonstrated to have a partner in her exercise of power is rightly seen to be compassionate.

With God's help, therefore, we have unbarred the imperial residence to an illustrious man of our family, who, descended from the race of the Amals, has a royal worthiness in his actions. He is patient in adversity, restrained in his prosperity, and possesses what is the most difficult kind of control: a self-control of long standing. His literary erudition adds to these good qualities, and excellently adorns an already praiseworthy nature. For it is through books that the prudent man discovers how he may become wiser. There the warrior finds how he may become staunch in his greatness of soul; there the prince learns in what manner he may control diverse peoples under an equal rule. No fortune in the world can exist that the glorious knowledge of literature does not enhance. . . .

Let us come to that most generous sobriety of his private life, which has amassed such an abundance of gifts, such a wealth of feasts, that in the light of his former activity he will be seen to require nothing further in conducting the realm. He is prompt in hospitality and most dutiful in compassion, so that although he has spent much, his worth has kept increasing through heaven's reward. . . .

Rejoice, then, Fathers of the Senate, and render thanks to the Heavenly Grace on our behalf, since I have ordained such a prince with me who will perform the good deeds that flow from our justice, and make his own good deeds manifest through his own sense of duty. For the virtue of his ancestors will admonish this man, and Theodoric as his uncle will effectually inspire him.

KEY DATES IN GOTHIC HISTORY

238 Goths raid Histria on the northwestern Black Sea coast

249 Goths under Guntheric and Argaith sack Marcianople

250 Goths under Cniva cross the Danube and sack Balkan cities

251 Cniva defeats a Roman army under the emperor Decius

268–269 seaborne Goths raid Asia Minor and Greece

270 Emperor Claudius II defeats Goths at Naissus

291 first mention of the Tervingi (after Diocletian's campaigns against them)

320s Goths dominate north side of the lower Danube

332 Constantine defeats and makes peace with the Tervingi

350 approximate date of Ulfila's translation of the Bible into Gothic

360s Athanaric becomes judge of the Tervingi

367–369 Emperor Valens campaigns in Gothia

around 370 Athanaric persecutes Gothic Christians

early 370s Huns defeat Ermanaric and his successor; many Greuthungi move west

376 Tervingi receive permission to settle in Roman Empire

377 Greuthungi cross the Danube; Fritigern begins Gothic revolt

378 Gothic victory at Battle of Adrianople

382 Theodosius I concludes a peace treaty with the Goths in the Balkans

395 Alaric leads a revolt and a series of raids in the Balkans

397 Stilicho leads expedition against Alaric; regent of Eastern Empire gives Alaric a high military post

399 rebellion of Goths led by Tribigild in Asia Minor

400 revolt of Gainas; mob violence against Goths in Constantinople

401 Alaric leads his followers to the Italian frontier

402 Alaric invades Italy, then retreats into the northwestern Balkans

Eagle brooches like this were usually worn in pairs, one on each shoulder.

405 Stilicho gives Alaric military command in the Balkans; Radagaisus invades Italy

406 Stilicho defeats Radagaisus and enslaves thousands of his followers

407 Alaric marches into Noricum and demands 4,000 pounds of gold

408 execution of Stilicho and massacre of the families of his barbarian auxiliaries; Alaric invades Italy

408–409 Alaric besieges Rome; escaped barbarian slaves flock to join his army

409 Alaric again besieges Rome

410 Alaric's troops sack Rome; he dies a couple months later

411 Athaulf leads the Goths into Gaul

415 Romans force the Goths into Spain; Athaulf murdered

416–418 Goths fight on Rome's behalf and are rewarded with lands in Gaul

418–451 reign of Theoderic I; his people become known as the Visigoths

451 Visigoths help defeat Attila's Huns

453 Death of Attila; eastern Goths begin to break away from Hun control

471–476 Visigoths under Euric take over most of southern Gaul

474 Theodoric the Amal becomes king of the Pannonian Goths

480s Euric repeatedly invades Spain

484 Theodoric unites the Pannonian and Thracian Goths

493 Theodoric becomes king of Italy

507 Visigoths lose most of their Gallic lands to the Franks

526 Theodoric succeeded by his daughter Amalsuntha

before 533 Cassiodorus writes his history of the Goths (now lost)

535–561 reconquest of Italy by Emperor Justinian

after 550 Jordanes writes his history of the Goths, based partly on Cassiodorus

711 Spanish Visigothic kingdom conquered by Arabs

A jeweled gold cross from Visigothic Spain

GLOSSARY

Asia Minor A large peninsula surrounded by the Mediterranean, Aegean, and Black seas. Also called Anatolia, it is the part of modern Turkey that lies in Asia.

auxiliaries In the Roman army, forces made up of non-Roman citizens from the provinces or from peoples with whom Rome had treaties.

Balkan Peninsula A peninsula surrounded by the Adriatic, Mediterranean, Aegean, and Black seas. Today it is occupied by the nations of Greece, Macedonia, Albania, Bosnia, Croatia, Slovenia, Yugoslavia, Bulgaria, part of Romania, and the European portion of Turkey.

cavalry Soldiers who fought on horseback.

Gaul The Roman name for the area between the Pyrenees Mountains, the Alps, and the Rhine River—modern France, Belgium, and Luxembourg; most of Switzerland; and the westernmost parts of Germany and of the Netherlands.

Germanic A language family that includes modern German, Dutch, English, Danish, Norwegian, and Swedish as well as the ancient forms of these languages and related languages, including Gothic; can also refer to peoples who spoke Germanic languages and to their culture.

mercenary A hired warrior, fighting for pay rather than out of loyalty to a nation or cause.

nomad A person whose livelihood depends on herding livestock from place to place according to the availability of water and pasture at different seasons.

Pannonia The Roman name for the part of Hungary west and south of the Danube River.

regent A person who governs on behalf of a monarch who is too young or too weak to rule.

Sarmatians A nomadic people from the region north of the Black Sea, whose language belonged to the Iranian language family (which includes modern Persian, Kurdish, Pashto, and Ossetic).

Scandinavia The northern European peninsula surrounded by the Arctic Ocean, North Sea, and Baltic Sea; in ancient times people thought it was an island. Today it is occupied by the nations of Norway and Sweden. The name can also refer to a larger region, which includes Denmark and Finland, too.

staple A crop that is heavily relied on, usually as a mainstay of the diet.

steppe A dry, flat grassland.

Thrace The ancient name for the region now occupied by Bulgaria and the European section of Turkey.

wattle-and-daub A method of construction in which thin, flexible branches are woven together to form a framework that is then filled in with a mixture of clay and straw.

FOR MORE INFORMATION

BOOKS

Markel, Rita J. *The Fall of the Roman Empire.* Minneapolis: Twenty-First Century Books, 2007.

Nardo, Don. *The Fall of the Roman Empire.* San Diego: Lucent Books, 2004.

Roberts, J. M. *Rome and the Classical West.* Vol. 3 of *The Illustrated History of the World.* New York: Oxford University Press, 2002.

Wilcox, Peter, and Rafael Treviño. *Barbarians Against Rome: Rome's Celtic, Germanic, Spanish, and Gallic Enemies.* Oxford: Osprey Publishing, 2000.

WEB SITES

British Museum. *The Domagnano Treasure.*
http://www.britishmuseum.org/explore/highlights/highlight_objects/
pe_mla/t/the_domagnano_treasure.aspx

Jordanes. *The Origin and Deeds of the Goths.* Translated by Charles C. Mierow.
http://www.acs.ucalgary.ca/~vandersp/Courses/texts/jordgeti.html

Judy, Tim. "The Treasure of the Pietroasa." *Vivid: Romania through International Eyes.*
http://www.vivid.ro/index.php/issue/77/page/artbeat/tstamp/0 and
http://www.vivid.ro/index.php/issue/78/page/artbeat/tstamp/
1143716354

Metropolitan Museum of Art. *Barbarians and Romans.*
http://www.metmuseum.org/toah/hd/barb/hd_barb.htm

Poznan Archaeological Museum. *Jewellery of the Goths.*
http://www.muzarp.poznan.pl/muzeum/muz_eng/wyst_czas/
Goci_katalog/index_kat.html

Spanish Fiestas. *Visigothic Spain.*
http://www.spanish-fiestas.com/history/visigoths.htm

SELECTED BIBLIOGRAPHY

Ammianus Marcellinus. *Roman History.* Translated by C. D. Yonge. Online at http://www.tertullian.org/fathers/
index.htm#Ammianus_Marcellinus

Barbero, Alessandro. *The Day of the Barbarians: The Battle that Led to the Fall of the Roman Empire.* Translated by John Cullen. New York: Walker, 2007.

Cunliffe, Barry, ed. *Prehistoric Europe: An Illustrated History.* New York: Oxford University Press, 1994.

Fletcher, Richard. *The Barbarian Conversion: From Paganism to Christianity*. New York: Henry Holt, 1997.

Heather, Peter. *The Fall of the Roman Empire: A New History of Rome and the Barbarians*. New York: Oxford, 2006.

———. *The Goths*. Malden, MA: Blackwell, 1998.

Jones, Terry, and Alan Ereira. *Terry Jones' Barbarians*. London: BBC Books, 2006.

Kulikowski, Michael. *Rome's Gothic Wars*. New York: Cambridge University Press, 2007.

McCullough, David Willis, ed. *Chronicles of the Barbarians: Firsthand Accounts of Pillage and Conquest, From the Ancient World to the Fall of Constantinople*. New York: Times Books, 1998.

Simons, Gerald. *Barbarian Europe*. New York: Time-Life Books, 1968.

Thiébaux, Marcelle. *The Writings of Medieval Women: An Anthology*. 2nd ed. New York: Garland, 1994.

Todd, Malcolm. *The Early Germans*. 2nd ed. Malden, MA: Blackwell Publishing, 2004.

Wolfram, Herwig. *History of the Goths*. Translated by Thomas J. Dunlap. Berkeley: University of California Press, 1988.

SOURCES FOR QUOTATIONS

Chapter 1

p. 10 "Now from this island": Heather, *The Goths*, pp. 11–12.

p. 10 "so the story": ibid., p. 28.

p. 15 "was at once surrounded": Kulikowski, *Rome's Gothic Wars*, p. 18.

p. 16 "the Roman provinces filled": Barbero, *The Day of the Barbarians*, p. 156.

p. 17 "Defeated by Aurelian": Wolfram, *History of the Goths*, p. 56.

p. 17 *pars Gothorum*: Kulikowski, *Rome's Gothic Wars*, p. 31.

p. 18 "better cause": Wolfram, *History of the Goths*, p. 58.

p. 18 *ripa Gothica*: Kulikowski, *Rome's Gothic Wars*, p. 76.

p. 19 "The Goths finally learned": ibid., p. 86.

p. 19 "treated our emperor": Barbero, *The Day of the Barbarians*, p. 22.

Chapter 2

p. 26 "They converted many": Fletcher, *The Barbarian Conversion*, p. 73.

p. 27 "bishop of the Christians": ibid., p. 73.

p. 27 "a tyrannical": ibid., p. 73.

p. 28 "He was the inventor": ibid., p. 77.

p. 28 "These books contain": Kulikowski, *Rome's Gothic Wars, p. 110.*

p. 28 "peace-loving and unwarlike": Wolfram, *History of the Goths*, p. 81.

p. 29 *"Atta unsar"*: Simons, *Barbarian Europe*, p. 17.

Chapter 3

p. 32 "the most powerful man": Ammianus Marcellinus, *Roman History* 27.V.6.

p. 32 "demanded back": Wolfram, *History of the Goths*, p. 66.

p. 33 "bound by a most dreadful" and "it would be unbecoming": Ammianus Marcellinus, *Roman History* 27.V.9.

p. 33 "Valens was so much": Heather, *The Fall of the Roman Empire,* p. 72.

p. 34 "a most warlike": Kulikowski, *Rome's Gothic Wars*, p. 112.

p. 34 "made a sudden": Ammianus Marcellinus, *Roman History* 31.III.1.

p. 34 "was astonished": ibid. 31.III.2.

p. 34 "gave himself up": Heather, *The Goths*, p. 98.

p. 35 "When Athanaric": Ammianus Marcellinus, *Roman History* 31.III.4–6.

p. 35 "The greater part": ibid. 31.III.8.

p. 35 "promising to live": ibid. 31.IV.1.

p. 36 "simply put": Barbero, *The Day of the Barbarians*, p. 43.

p. 37 "those detested generals": Ammianus Marcellinus, *Roman History* 31.IV.11.

p. 37 "to allow time": ibid. 31.V.4.

p. 38 "When Lupicinus learned": Heather, *The Fall of the Roman Empire,* pp.164–165.

p. 39 "spread over every": ibid., p. 173.

p. 39 "descending from the mountains": Ammianus Marcellinus, *Roman History* 31.XII.17.

p. 40 "were entirely beaten": ibid. 31.XIII.7.

p. 40 "Philanthropy has prevailed": Barbero, *The Day of the Barbarians*, p. 133.

p. 40 "This is not": Heather, *The Fall of the Roman Empire*, p. 190.

Chapter 4

p. 44 "were paramount": Kulikowski, *Rome's Gothic Wars*, p. 156.

p. 44 "a barbarian by birth": Barbero, *The Day of the Barbarians*, p. 143.

p. 45 "Only a madman": ibid., p. 140.

p. 46 "when one dressed": ibid., pp. 140–141.

p. 46 "Just as in the past": ibid., p. 138.

p. 48 "They immediately began": Jones, *Terry Jones' Barbarians*, p. 123.

p. 52 "Alaric did not": Heather, *The Fall of the Roman Empire*, p. 226.

p. 53 "The whole world": Jones, *Terry Jones' Barbarians*, p. 130.

p. 54 "Rome, the mistress": ibid., p. 131.

p. 54 "They set fire": McCullough, *Chronicles of the Barbarians*, p. 144.

p. 55 "Now you must" and "Romans and barbarians": Jones, *Terry Jones' Barbarians*, p. 131.

p. 55 "If any mental": Heather, *The Fall of the Roman Empire*, p. 235.

p. 55 "Let thy [Rome's]": ibid., p. 234.

Chapter 5

p. 57 "It seems that": Heather, *The Fall of the Roman Empire*, p. 239.

p. 58 "with all the honour": Jones, *Terry Jones' Barbarians*, p. 131.

p. 58 "Placidia, dressed in royal": Heather, *The Fall of the Roman Empire*, p. 240.

p. 59 "on behalf": Wolfram, *History of the Goths*, p. 171.

p. 59 "land for farming": Heather, *The Goths*, p. 182.

p. 60 "Hand to hand": Simons, *Barbarian Europe*, p. 40.

p. 61 "Becoming aware": Heather, *The Goths*, p. 189.

p. 62 "The party of the Goths": Heather, *The Fall of the Roman Empire*, pp. 358–359.

p. 63 "While remaining": Heather, *The Goths*, p. 160.

p. 64 "by Divine help": ibid., p. 221.

p. 66 "After mourning": Thiébaux, *The Writings of Medieval Women*, pp. 80–82.

INDEX

Page numbers for illustrations are in boldface

ABOUT THE AUTHOR

Kathryn Hinds grew up near Rochester, New York. She studied music and writing at Barnard College, and went on to do graduate work in comparative literature and medieval studies at the City University of New York. She has written more than forty books for young people, including *Everyday Life in Medieval Europe* and the books in the series LIFE IN THE MEDIEVAL MUSLIM WORLD, LIFE IN ELIZABETHAN ENGLAND, LIFE IN ANCIENT EGYPT, LIFE IN THE ROMAN EMPIRE, and LIFE IN THE RENAISSANCE. Kathryn lives in the north Georgia mountains with her husband, their son, and an assortment of cats and dogs. When she is not reading or writing, she enjoys dancing, gardening, knitting, playing music, and taking walks in the woods. Visit Kathryn online at www.kathrynhinds.com